Being Anxious
Help For Social Anxiety

David Tuffley

To my beloved Nation of Four
Concordia Domi – Foris Pax

"It's not all bad. Heightened self-consciousness, apartness, an inability to join in, physical shame and self-loathing—they are not all bad. Those devils have been my angels. Without them I would never have disappeared into language, literature, the mind, laughter and all the mad intensities that made and unmade me." — Stephen Fry

Published 2014, 2021 by Altiora Publications
AltioraPublications.com/

ISBN-13: 978-1505378092 ISBN-10: 1505378095

About the Author
David Tuffley PhD is a Lecturer in Applied Ethics & Socio-Technical Studies at Griffith University in Australia. David has written widely on Applied Psychology topics.

Facebook: www.facebook.com/tuffley/

Acknowledgements

I acknowledge the work of Abraham Maslow, Martin Seligman and Howard Gardner.

Also the *Turrbal* and *Jagera* indigenous peoples, on whose ancestral land I write this book. This ancient continent has a profound story for those who would listen.

Contents

INTRODUCTION 1

CHAPTER 1: UNDERSTANDING SOCIAL ANXIETY 2

THE WORLD IS NOT AS DANGEROUS AS IT ONCE WAS 2
THE CARROT AND THE STICK 3
WE DID NOT EVOLVE SURROUNDED BY MILLIONS OF STRANGERS....................... 4
PHOBIAS ARE NATURAL INSTINCTS TAKEN TOO FAR...................................... 5
SYMPTOMS OF SOCIAL ANXIETY 6
THINKING STYLES THAT INTENSIFY SOCIAL PHOBIA 7
YOU ARE NOT ALONE 8

CHAPTER 2: COGNITIVE BEHAVIOUR THERAPY (CBT)....................10

MINDFULNESS.. 11
RESTRUCTURING YOUR THOUGHT PATTERNS 12

CHAPTER 3: EXPOSURE THERAPY...14

CHAPTER 4: FACE YOUR FEARS 17

HIERARCHY OF FEAR 17

CHAPTER 5: YOUR ASSOCIATES 19

CHAPTER 6: LIFESTYLE 21

CHAPTER 7: MEDICATION FOR SOCIAL ANXIETY 23

CHAPTER 8: GENERALISED ANXIETY DISORDER (GAD) 25

SYMPTOMS OF GAD.. 26
THERAPY FOR GAD 27

CONCLUSION 28

ABOUT THE AUTHOR 29

Introduction

Upwards of 20% of people in developed countries suffer from Social Anxiety, and many of them have had it since they were children. For these many millions whose lives are seriously curtailed by the crippling fear of social situations, this book can definitely help.

Being Anxious: Help for Social Anxiety gives you practical, down-to-earth advice on what Social Anxiety is, what causes it and how you can deal with it.

In this no-nonsense how-to guide you will get a set of *Cognitive Behaviour Therapies* that have been proven to work with a generation of sufferers. – use them, safe in the knowledge that these have already worked for countless people already, people who now live richer, more satisfying lives.

Chapter 1: Understanding Social Anxiety

Social anxiety (or social phobia) is the debilitating fear of interacting with people. At its heart is the belief that you are being negatively judged, which leads you to avoid those situations where being judged is a possibility. To make matters worse, it is a self-reinforcing fear in which the more often you avoid situations, the more established and habitual the fear of negative judgment becomes.

You can understand the nature of social anxiety by seeing it in its evolutionary perspective. In our evolutionary past, strangers *were* dangerous. Being wary of them helped us to survive. There were the family and close friends inside our circle of trust, and then there was everyone else. There was only ever 'us and them'.

The world is not as dangerous as it once was

The foundation for dealing with social anxiety is to understand at a *rational* level that in today's world we do not need to be so scared of strangers. As dangerous as they might once have been, today they are less dangerous. To watch the news on TV or read the newspapers, you could be forgiven for thinking that the world is a dangerous place indeed, but that is a distortion of reality. Every year the world becomes a little safer and more civilised as Stephen Pinker points out in his 2011 book *The Better Angels of Our Nature: Why Violence Has Declined.*

Rigorously enforced laws that guarantee individual rights have seen to that. We all know that if we attack someone we will find ourselves incarcerated with a criminal record. We have learned to restrain our violent impulses. On the rare occasion when someone *does* become violent, often under the influence of inhibition-reducing alcohol, they are publicly shamed on TV news and sent to jail or made to pay a hefty fine.

The carrot and the stick

Since Roman times, violent offenders have been put in prison where they cannot breed. At the same time, altruistic behaviour is rewarded by society. This carrot and stick approach is gradually reducing the overall proportion of people with violent tendencies in the general population, while increasing the proportion of helpful, well-intentioned people. This process has been on-going for nearly 2,000 years, which represents roughly 6,000 generations of people.

3

I am not suggesting that violence does not still occur in the world, only that it is gradually declining, a fact which is proven by the hard evidence presented by Professor Pinker.

We did not evolve surrounded by millions of strangers

We do not need to fear strangers in the way our ancestors did 10,000+ years ago. In those days, people lived in small nomadic groups, very often a single multi-generational family group. Everyone knew everyone else. Children were raised by the community. There were no towns or cities, much less the mega-cities of today. Even though we evolved as small group dwellers, the reality of life today in the 21st Century is that more than half of the world's population lives in cities where you live surrounded by millions of strangers. This is always going to be stressful for people in whom the age-old instinctive fear of strangers is still strong.

If you suffer from social anxiety, it is helpful to understand that what you have is a natural instinct that is being outraged by the conditions of modern life. The instinct is over-reacting; the perceived danger has become blown out of proportion to the actual danger. You are not defective; you just need to dial back the instinctive reaction to a more rational level.

You can take a big step towards overcoming your social anxiety by activating your rational, logical mind and coming to understand the truth of modern city life. Watching Stephen Pinker's TED Talk is a good start. Our instincts tell us to be afraid of everyone we don't know, and while some of those strangers should definitely be treated as potentially dangerous, the vast majority of strangers are normal, civilised people who would not dream of harming you.

Phobias are natural instincts taken too far

Mild social anxiety is in itself a natural enough phenomenon. It becomes a problem when it crosses the line and becomes an unreasonable curb upon your freedom to live your life fully. Any phobia comes about when a natural survival instinct is taken to an unreasonable extreme.

Avoiding being shut into a tight space is natural, but claustrophobia takes this too far. Being wary of spiders can save your life, but arachnophobia can cripple you in the presence of a harmless spider. Falling from a high place can kill you, but acrophobia makes you avoid any high place regardless of how safe it is to be there. People you don't know and trust can be dangerous, so being wary of them is a good idea, but social phobia takes this healthy instinct too far.

Symptoms of Social Anxiety

How do you know if what you are feeling is Social Anxiety? The symptoms fall into three distinct categories; *Emotional, Physical and Behavioural.*

Emotional symptoms include being overly self-conscious in everyday social situations, being worried about an upcoming social event, worrying that people are scrutinising and judging you, worrying that you will do something foolish and embarrass yourself, worrying that others will see that you are anxious, that they will notice your nervous demeanour and think you're an idiot.

Physical symptoms include blushing, gasping for breath, stomach cramps and nausea, trembling, including quavering voice, rapidly beating heart, sweating or hot flushes and feeling faint.

Behavioural symptoms include avoiding social contact, keeping a low-profile or staying in the background to avoid notice, needing to have a trusted friend to come with you, and consuming alcohol or other drugs before social situations to settle your nerves.

Thinking styles that intensify social phobia

When a sufferer becomes anxious about a social situation, they adopt a thinking style tends to intensify the problem, and which justifies to themselves the growing feeling of dread. Mindfulness (discussed later) helps you to become conscious of these thought patterns. When you notice yourself thinking this way, you can then make a conscious effort to replace the negative thought for a positive one.

Mind reading – you mistakenly believe that you know what everyone is thinking; they are thinking the same negative thoughts as you, seeing you in the same negative way that you see yourself. Counter this with the rational thought that *"they are pre-occupied with their own thoughts and needs. If they think of me at all, it is probably only in passing'.*

Foreseeing the future – you are sure that things will turn out really badly. You can see the future and it is not good. Counter this with the rational thought that *'worst case scenarios almost never happen. The likelihood is that the situation will go OK, often better than OK'.*

Catastrophizing – an aspect of the previous point, you exaggerate the situation to the worst possible outcome. The rationale for doing this is to prepare yourself for the worst. *Counter this with the rational thought that the worst case almost never happens (as previously) and that expecting the worst is to invite the*

7

worst. If you feel it is necessary anticipate negative outcomes, it is better to plan for and expect the best but also have a plan ready if the worst happens.

Personalizing – you mistakenly believe that people are focussing on your negative aspects and judging you. Or that what is going on with other people is due to you personally. Or worse, they know it is due to you and they hate you for it. Counter this with the rational thought that *very little of what goes on with other people has to do with you personally. Remind yourself that by being quiet and relaxed that you are more likely to see and understand what is really going on in the world around you. By being a neutral presence, you are not causing any reactions and this allows you to clearly see and understand the reality of situations.*

You are not alone

There may be some comfort in knowing that you are not alone. Social anxiety is in fact the most common anxiety experienced by people. As mentioned in the 4th Edition of the *Diagnostic and Statistical Manual of Mental Disorders* (DSM-IV) Social Anxiety Disorder is experienced by around 20% of Americans at some point in their life. This figure is likely to be similar elsewhere in the developed world.

Half of that 20% have developed the disorder by age 11, while 80% of sufferers have it well-established by the time they are 20. Childhood is obviously a vulnerable time where those struggling with anxiety are more likely than others to develop depressive illnesses, patterns of drug abuse and other psychological problems.

The good news is that Psychology has developed a range of effective therapies for the treatment of social anxiety. These will be discussed in detail in the chapters that follow.

Chapter 2:
Cognitive Behaviour
Therapy (CBT)

CBT is the general name for the kind of therapy that aims to change the way you think and act. It is an effective therapy for helping sufferers of a range of problems, including social anxiety to overcome their fears and live a fuller life.

CBT comes in two parts; the cognitive component where you examine and restructure the way you are thinking about a situation that causes anxiety, and the behavioral component – how your actions have been causing anxiety, and how you can reduce anxiety by acting differently. Action follows thought, so the therapy starts with becoming aware of how you are currently thinking.

The mind is habit-driven. We develop patterns of thinking that become established as habits over time. In the same way that flowing water wears a deeper and wider channel as time goes by, so too do our mental habits make more established neural pathways in our brains. Just as it is possible to alter the course of a stream by redirecting the water, it is also possible to change established thought patterns and their neural pathways.

Changing a habitual way of thinking is not an easy thing to do. With sustained effort though, CBT can systematically change those troublesome thought patterns. It is not quick fix, but it *does* work.

CBT takes a practical, problem-solving approach in which specific trigger points are identified. Once you know what these points are, you shine the light of logic and reason upon them. You keep the spotlight on the problem until you are able to re-frame the thought in a more constructive way. This is how you unlearn your existing habits and replace them with new ones that are easier to live with.

Mindfulness

Present moment focus (otherwise known as mindfulness) is a key element of CBT. There is nothing mysterious or mystical about mindfulness, it is simply a state of *heightened present moment awareness* where you monitor the thought-patterns running through your mind. Mindfulness is an essential skill for becoming more self-aware and personal growth; in terms of CBT though, you are looking for the thoughts that trigger an anxious mood.

By focussing on your thoughts in the present moment, you are able to snap out of the habit of worrying about the past and the future. Your attention is on the here and now, which is the only real time and place that you have in life.

Restructuring your thought patterns

In CBT, the key is to raise your awareness of the anxiety-producing thoughts that are causing you problems. You then challenge them like you would an overbearing associate who is used to bossing you about. Then you can actively replace those troublesome thoughts with something more positive and realistic. Try doing this:

Become aware of your negative thoughts. These are usually what are going through your mind just before that feeling of dread started to take hold of you. Unless you make the conscious effort to identify these thoughts they will probably pass through and be gone without you even being aware of them. Once the anxiety sets in, thoughts are replaced by the feelings that were triggered by the thought.

Anxiety sufferers often perceive situations as being worse than they actually are. For example you might feel that when you are in a room full of people at a social gathering that everyone is looking at you, judging every little thing about you from the clothes you are wearing to the way you are standing and the expression on your face. *'Everyone is staring at me ...'* might be the thought that runs quickly through your mind that triggers the anxious feelings.

Challenge your negative thoughts. This second step is about using *logic* to refute the anxiety-producing thought that you identified in the previous step. Rationality has to triumph over irrationality.

Taking a deep breath and repeating a calming mantra to help you relax, you question what evidence there might be that, for example, everyone is staring at you. In questioning, you look around the room and notice that in fact no-one is looking at you, except for perhaps that one person who glanced your way a few seconds earlier. Logic suggests that people will be looking at their conversation partners, not at you. Scientists are rational creatures; so imagine yourself to be a scientist testing the hypothesis that everyone is staring at you. You question the evidence that produced those frightening thoughts, then you analyse and test the truth of those negative thoughts.

Exchange the negative for the positive. Having gone through the rational process of testing the truth of those negative thoughts and found them to be false or at least exaggerated, you then deliberately replace them with positive, rational thoughts. For example, once you identified the negative thought *(everyone's staring at me)* then refuted it *(I've looked around and actually they are not staring at me)* you replace the negative thought with a positive, rational thought *(I'm fitting in here as well as anyone, fact is most of these folks will be feeling anxious too, that's why people drink alcohol. I'm going to relax, lower my expectations about what should happen and just go with the flow … it is going to be fine!)*

Chapter 3:
Exposure Therapy

Used in conjunction with CBT or by itself, exposure therapy helps you to master your fear by exposing you to a graded set of fear-inducing situations, beginning with very mild, and progressing to the next, slightly more fearful situation, mastering that and so on all the way up to the ultimate terror.

With social anxiety, this might begin with a casual hello to your next door neighbour, and progress in stages to asking a stranger at the shopping mall for the time, striking up a conversation with the person next to you on a plane or train (usually best done close to the end of the journey), all the way up to going to a bar or a party and talking to attractive strangers.

Try this three step process to progressively de-sensitise yourself of fear:

Relax & Breathe. At the heart of most relaxation techniques is a simple three stage process. First, with full conscious awareness take ten deep breaths, in through the nose, out through the mouth, using the diaphragm and not your ribcage to fill your lungs. Don't be in a hurry to finish, savour every breath and take simple pleasure in the fact that you are alive and there is air to breath. Second, on the out-breath silently say to yourself *'I am relaxed'* – don't just say it though, you have to *feel it*. Third, when you have finished your breaths, actively see yourself fearlessly doing the thing that you previously felt afraid of. Make this image as vivid in your imagination as you can, turn it into a movie if that helps. Just see it happening and believe that if you can imagine it in your inside world, you can perform in the outside world.

This is a powerful technique that is used by high performing, successful individuals in all walks of life from Prime Ministers and Presidents to Navy SEALs.

Make your list. List out 10 to 20 fear-inducing situations that take you to your final goal of doing something terrifying that you really want or need to be able to do. If your goal is to make a really persuasive speech to a room full of people, begin by looking at photos of people doing just that. See Steve Jobs launching the first iPhone, or Martin Luther King delivering his I have a dream speech or whatever inspiration speech you like. The end of the list has you standing before an audience of a thousand people. The spotlight is on you, you are dynamic and persuasive and crowd loves every word. When you finish they give you a standing ovation.

Work through the list. Using the relaxation technique outlined in the first step above, work your way through the list from easy to hard. Stay in each scary situation for as long as it takes to feel the fear subside. You will need to repeat the relaxation technique often. It is the best way to master the fear. The whole process is likely to take hours and it should not be rushed. Do not expect to finish it quickly, and *do* expect to have to repeat each step several times until you feel quite comfortable.

Chapter 4:
Face your fears

As difficult as it might seem, often the simple act of making the decision to not run from your fears any more, to turn and face them, can be a powerfully transformative moment. It is an act of courage that can pay big dividends. 'Avoidance', as Psychologists call it, can keep you locked in a downward spiral. The longer it goes on, the worse the anxiety becomes.

If you can find the courage to face your fears, to deliberately and defiantly place yourself in the very situation(s) that make you anxious, if you can use the thought-restructuring techniques and breathing/relaxation techniques to stay cool calm and collected, then you will have made a giant step towards controlling your fear instead of the fear controlling you.

Hierarchy of fear

Earlier we discussed the technique of making a list of situations that are likely to cause anxiety, structured with the mildest challenge at the beginning and progressing through 15 or more stages to the scariest, most stressful scenario. This is sometimes called a 'hierarchy of fear' and it works by progressively desensitizing you to stressful situations and lessening your anxiety.

The key to this technique is to manage your expectations as to how fast it will work. It takes time, and it is necessary to be patient. Each step must be taken by concentrating on reducing your anxiety using the breathing and relaxation techniques.

Approach the nerve-wracking business of facing your fears in the full knowledge that it is within your abilities to overcome the debilitating fears that have been controlling your life.

For example, if meeting strangers makes you anxious, you could start going to a party with an extraverted friend. Practice the rational thinking and breathing relaxation to become comfortable with this challenge, repeating until you have become comfortable with it. Then you can progress to introducing yourself to a stranger and so on.

Remember, patience and persistence is the key to success with this technique. The process will take as long as it takes, and that is OK. After all, you are re-routing the neural pathways I your brain and that is not a quick process.

Chapter 5:
Your Associates

It is a fact of human nature that we become like the people we associate with. The more time we spend in someone's company, the more like them we become and vice versa. This tendency is hard-wired into the human species, largely because in our evolutionary past, survival depended on having a support group around you. The world was a dangerous place, and loners were vulnerable.

To help remedy social anxiety, seek out and join supportive social groups, people who share your values and interests, people who encourage your dreams.

Enrol in a social skills class. Your local community college or other community group run courses for people wanting to improve their social skills, including becoming more assertive. Courses like these operate in a non-judgmental environment where you can safely grow.

Volunteer for a worthy cause. Your local community newspaper lists the various groups in the area where you live and the causes they represent. If any of these appeal to you, consider joining the group and involve yourself in their efforts. There is great satisfaction to be had in finding a cause that is greater than you and devoting yourself to it. When you find a group of people with a common cause and immerse yourself, the anxiety melts away.

Improve your communication skills. Even the best speakers and writers put effort into improving their skills, so there is no shame in seeking to become a better communicator. It is a life-long journey. Your aim should be to develop clear, emotionally-mature communication. Being able to connect with people at the emotional level is the key to developing good relationships.

Chapter 6:
Lifestyle

A healthy lifestyle is an invaluable support to the treatment of social anxiety. Consider making some changes along the following lines:

Reduce your caffeine intake. Caffeinated drinks of all sorts (coffee, tea, caffeinated soda, energy drinks) as well as chocolate are stimulants that can increase anxiety if you become over-stimulated.

Drink alcohol in moderation. As tempting as it might be to self-medicate with a few stiff drinks, the reality is that too much alcohol can increase the likelihood of having an anxiety attack. Since alcohol lowers your inhibitions, it is easy to have a few too many and wind up worse than you started.

Reduce or stop smoking. Nicotine is a stimulant which can have an apparently calming effect on your nerves, but in reality can lead to higher, not lower levels of anxiety in the longer term.

Exercise. Physical activity is a natural anti-anxiety treatment. Try to get half an hour of aerobic activity most days, or every day if you can manage it.

Get enough sleep. Your nervous system is more vulnerable when it is sleep deprived. Over time, if you are not getting enough sleep your ability to cope with

21

situations will be compromised. You cannot think clearly when you are sleep deprived clear thinking is an important part of overcoming social anxiety.

Addiction. It is not unusual for people with social anxiety to develop addictions of one kind or another, with alcohol being the most common. Alcohol is, after all, a socially acceptable drug that is not just tolerated but encouraged in many circles. Moderate consumption is not normally a problem, but for a number of reasons there are people (the socially anxious among them) who find that they cannot stop at one or two drinks. For these, the old saying is true, that *'one drink is too much, a hundred drinks is not enough'*. See Beating Addiction for a good self-help guide'

Chapter 7: Medication for social anxiety

Cognitive Behavior Therapy offers the best long-term prospect of a cure for social anxiety. In severe cases it may be beneficial to obtain short-term relief for acute symptoms of social anxiety. Medication alone does not normally offer a permanent cure, only relief from the suffering you are feeling right now. It can however be used in conjunction with CBT.

These are all matters to be decided in consultation with your health care professional.

Three types of medication are used in the treatment of social anxiety:

Beta blockers – useful for relieving performance anxiety - they work by inhibiting the adrenaline that produces the fight or flight response. Beta blockers do not reduce the anxiety as such; they just control the physical symptoms like shaking hands or quavering voice, sweating, blushing and rapid heartbeat.

Antidepressants –helpful with severe cases where a person is crippled by social anxiety. Paxil, Effexor, and Zoloft have been approved by the U.S. Food and Drug Administration for the treatment of social phobia.

Benzodiazepines – fast-acting anti-anxiety medications (eg. Valium). Benzodiazepines are both sedating and addictive, so they are usually only prescribed when other medications have not worked.

Chapter 8: Generalised Anxiety Disorder (GAD)

The difference between GAD and Social Anxiety Disorder (SAD) is the *pervasiveness* of worry and anxiety with GAD, whereas with SAD, the anxiety usually only in social situations.

GAD sufferers feel tense and nervous most of the time; there is a general sense of worry about almost everything, a free-floating dread that provides the backdrop of their life and colours everything they think and do.

The subject of their worries can be the same as non-GAD folk (i.e. money, health, relationships, work) but it is escalated to a much higher level of intensity. Relaxation becomes difficult or impossible. It interferes with their sleep, drains their energy and wears them out. The chronic stress causes their immune system to work less efficiently so they are more likely to suffer from chronic illnesses; like never seeming to shake off that flu from a month ago or something more serious.

Symptoms of GAD

Symptoms of GD include the following:

Emotional symptoms of GAD include:

- Incessant worries running through your mind
- Feeling like your anxiety is out of control, unstoppable
- Intrusive thoughts about worrisome things and you cannot make them stop
- Uncertainty avoidance - you need to know what will happen
- Pervasive feeling of dread

Behavioural symptoms of GAD include:

- Cannot relax or enjoy quiet time by yourself
- Cannot concentrate
- Procrastination due to feeling overwhelmed
- Avoiding situations that make you anxious

Physical symptoms of GAD include:

- Muscle tension, aches and pains caused by chronic tension (eg. neck pain)
- Insomnia
- Restless, on-edge, fidgety
- Digestive upset; ulcer, nausea, diarrhoea

Therapy for GAD

Understand what worry really is. Many GAD sufferers fundamentally believe that their worries are caused by people and events *outside* of themselves – which means they have little or no real control over those external agents and therefore powerless to stop the worry.

The truth is that *between what happens to you and how you react to it lays your power to choose.* This was the powerful truth that Victor Frankl wrote about so movingly in Man's Search For Meaning. The external triggers do not *have* to cause worry. The worry happens due to a largely unconscious habit where you react in a particular way that causes the worry.

By using the same mindfulness and restructuring techniques outlined in the Cognitive Behaviour Therapy chapter, you can become aware of how the trigger works, and by staying relaxed you can face it logically, decide that it is irrational and re-program the way you think about the whole issue. In short, you can consciously choose a new and better way of thinking.

Conclusion

Social Anxiety Disorder and its more pervasive form *Generalised Anxiety Disorder* can exercise a crippling influence of the lives of sufferers who may have laboured under its tyrannical control since they were children.

This concise eBook tries to give suffers and interested others two things;

An **understanding** of the nature of the condition, its evolutionary origins and how it works, and

A set of **Cognitive Behaviour Therapies** that have been proven to work with a generation of sufferers – you can use them with confidence, safe in the knowledge that it has already worked with countless people already, people who know live richer more satisfying lives.

Best of luck on your journey!

The End

About the Author

David Tuffley PhD is a Senior Lecturer in Applied Ethics & Socio-Technical Studies at Griffith University in Australia. David has written widely on applied Psychology topics.

Join him on Facebook at **facebook.com/tuffley**